THE GREAT PACIFIC
GARBAGE PATCH

By Laura Perdew

ECOLOGICAL **DISASTERS**

Content Consultant
Dr. Angelicque "Angel" White
Associate Professor
CEOAS, Oregon State University

Essential Library

abdopublishing.com

Published by Abdo Publishing, a division of ABDO, PO Box 398166, Minneapolis, Minnesota 55439. Copyright © 2018 by Abdo Consulting Group, Inc. International copyrights reserved in all countries. No part of this book may be reproduced in any form without written permission from the publisher. Essential Library™ is a trademark and logo of Abdo Publishing.

Printed in the United States of America, North Mankato, Minnesota
042017
092017

Cover Photo: Peter Bennett/Ambient Images/Newscom
Interior Photos: Peter Bennett/Ambient Images/Newscom, 4, 22–23, 28, 31, 81; Andrew Payne/Alamy, 7; NOAA, 9; iStockphoto, 10–11, 12, 13, 16–17, 21, 26, 27, 32, 34, 40–41, 42, 48–49, 56, 69, 89, 93, 95, 98 (bottom right), 99 (bottom); Alex Kolokythas Photography/Shutterstock Images, 14; Everett Historical/ Shutterstock Images, 18; Bali Padma/iStockphoto, 20; Steve Ringman/KRT/Newscom, 35; N. Nehring/iStockphoto, 38; Shutterstock Images, 39, 43, 90–91, 99 (top); Roberta Olenick/All Canada Photos/Glow Images, 45; Kao Lao/iStockphoto, 51; Robert Neumann/Shutterstock Images, 52–53; Yvette Cardozo/Alamy, 58; Steve Cordory/Shutterstock Images, 59; Remko de Waal/ANP/Newscom, 60–61, 64; The Ocean Cleanup, 63, 73; Francis R. Malasig/EPA/Newscom, 66–67; Juan Monino/iStockphoto, 70; Albert Karimov/Shutterstock Images, 74, 98 (left); Tyler Olson/Shutterstock Images, 77, 98 (top right); Nitikorn Poonsiri/ Shutterstock Images, 83; Gaurav Gadani/iStockphoto, 84–85; Slobodan Miljevic/iStockphoto, 86; Essential Image/Shutterstock Images, 88; Kirin Photo/ iStockphoto, 96

Editor: Heather Hudak
Series Designer: Laura Polzin

Publisher's Cataloging-in-Publication Data

Names: Perdew, Laura, author.
Title: The great Pacific garbage patch / by Laura Perdew.
Description: Minneapolis, MN : Abdo Publishing, 2018. | Series: Ecological
    disasters | Includes bibliographical references and index.
Identifiers: LCCN 2016962235 | ISBN 9781532110238 (lib. bdg.) |
    ISBN 9781680788082 (ebook)
Subjects: LCSH: Waste disposal in the ocean--Juvenile literature. | Plastic marine
    debris--Juvenile literature. | Marine pollution--Juvenile literature. | Refuse and
    refuse disposal--Juvenile literature. | Environmental degradation--Juvenile
    literature. | Ecological disturbances--Juvenile literature.
Classification: DDC 363.739--dc23
LC record available at http://lccn.loc.gov/2016962235

CONTENTS

Captain Charles Moore has spent countless hours collecting plastic samples in the waters of the North Pacific Ocean.

ONE

THE GREAT PACIFIC GARBAGE PATCH

On an August day in 1997, Captain Charles Moore was sailing the Pacific Ocean from Hawaii to California through a generally calm weather system called the North Pacific subtropical high. By taking this route, he hoped to avoid dangerous weather farther south. Moore had recently completed a transpacific race and was returning to California. As he sailed across the sea, he expected calm winds and a glassy surface. Instead, he noticed a bit of trash. He didn't think much of it until he saw another piece of trash. And then he saw even more trash.

NORTH PACIFIC SUBTROPICAL HIGH

The North Pacific subtropical high is an area of high pressure over the northern part of the Pacific Ocean. In high-pressure systems, storms and moisture are diverted around the area. Dense air sinks and warms, leaving areas with weak winds and sluggish ocean currents. This part of the ocean was typically avoided by seafarers because it is so calm— somewhat of an ocean desert. It lies along the same latitudes as some of the world's great deserts that are similarly affected by high atmospheric pressure.

What disturbed Moore most was that he was hundreds of miles from shore. This far out, the ocean should have been pristine. Instead, Moore saw bottles, bottle caps, wrappers, fishing nets, scraps of film, and other bits of floating plastic. "It seemed unbelievable," Moore recounted.[1]

In many parts of the world, it is common for trash to litter streets, sidewalks, and parks. Even in ports and on beaches, litter is not uncommon. But for Moore, who grew up sailing and swimming in the ocean, the deep sea was the one place that had always been free of human detritus. That there was debris so far from land in a remote part of the ocean bothered Moore so profoundly that he couldn't stop thinking about it. Looking back at his logbook from the voyage, Moore read notes about seeing trash for seven consecutive days. In that time, his crew had covered more than 1,000 nautical miles (1,850 km). Moore had come across an accumulation of debris, a "garbage patch," that had been predicted a decade earlier by scientists.[2] It later came to be known as the Great Pacific Garbage Patch.

WHAT IS THE GREAT PACIFIC GARBAGE PATCH?

The Great Pacific Garbage Patch is in the North Pacific Ocean. It is a collection of marine debris that is the result of rotating ocean currents between Japan and the United States.

Most of the plastics and trash in the Great Pacific Garbage Patch will not break down over time.

> "A lot of people hear the word 'patch' and they immediately think of almost like a blanket of trash that can easily be scooped up, but actually these areas are always moving and changing with the currents, and it's mostly these tiny plastics that you can't immediately see with the naked eye."[4]
>
> —*Dianna Parker, NOAA Marine Debris Program, June 2014*

TRAPPED IN ARCTIC ICE

Ocean currents have taken debris as far as the Arctic, where micro plastics have been found frozen in the ice. Recent studies of the ice have found hundreds of particles trapped in 35 cubic feet (1 cu m). This is a much greater concentration of plastic than in the Great Pacific Garbage Patch. Moreover, as the ice melts, it releases the plastics back into the ocean. Researchers from Dartmouth College estimated that 1 trillion bits of micro plastics could be freed from the ice by 2024.[5]

These rotating currents, called gyres, are like giant whirlpools that concentrate the debris in one area. The Great Pacific Garbage Patch is actually composed of two separate patches—the Eastern Garbage Patch and the Western Garbage Patch. The eastern patch is located between Hawaii and the mainland United States, while the western patch is off the coast of Japan. These two patches are connected by the North Pacific Subtropical Gyre, a large area of 7.7 million square miles (20 million sq km) where several Pacific currents interact.[3] In this convergence zone where winds from different areas meet, the massive circular current moves in a clockwise direction. Over the span of years, it can take debris from Japan to the United States and back again. No one knows exactly the size of the garbage patch in the Pacific.

It is important to understand that the Great Pacific Garbage Patch is not an island or a raft of trash bound together, nor is it confined to a specific point. It is simply an area where debris is concentrated and freely floating through the ocean. Further, it is not visible from the air or by satellite because most of the debris is below the surface of the water, and much of the collection is made up of micro debris. Often, people

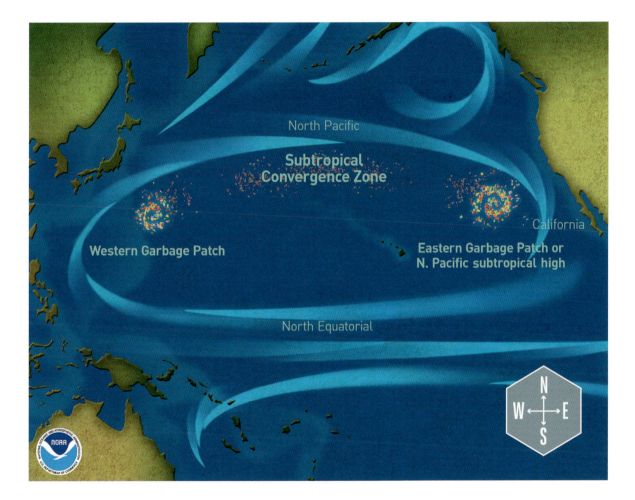

Wind and waves help spread garbage over large areas in the Great Pacific Garbage Patch, though little of it can be seen by the naked eye.

traveling through the garbage patch cannot see the scale of the collection. Captain Charles Moore likened the Great Pacific Garbage Patch to a bowl of soup: "It was and is a thin plastic soup, a soup lightly seasoned with plastic flakes, bulked out here and there with 'dumplings': buoys, net clumps, floats, crates, and other 'macro debris.'"[6]

Parts of the North Pacific subtropical high are so calm that mariners called the area "the horse latitudes."[7] If sailors were caught in the stagnant currents with low winds, they often had to dump horses or other livestock overboard to lighten their load and conserve fresh drinking water until the winds increased enough to resume sailing.

Other types of marine debris in the Great Pacific Garbage Patch and other garbage patches around the world include plastic bags, rubber tires, paper, metals, derelict fishing gear, abandoned ships, Styrofoam, textiles, and more. These items can be found on the surface of the

Trash dumped into the ocean far from land eventually makes its way to beaches and shorelines.

OTHER GARBAGE PATCHES

The Great Pacific Garbage Patch is not the only garbage patch in Earth's oceans—it is just the most notorious. There are other places in the oceans where currents converge in much the same manner as in the North Pacific Ocean. In the Atlantic Ocean, for example, the North Atlantic subtropical convergence zone consists of two gyres that have formed the Atlantic Garbage Patch. Located several hundred miles east of North America, the patch traps marine debris in its currents. Researchers studying the Atlantic patch trawled the surface of the ocean and found more than 520,000 bits of trash per square mile (2.59 sq km).[11] A patch was also discovered in the Indian Ocean, approximately halfway between Australia and Africa.

ocean or littering the ocean floor. Of all the debris in garbage patches, 90 percent is plastic in all shapes and sizes.[8] Much of this consists of micro plastics, tiny pieces of plastic less than 0.2 inches (5 mm) in size.[9] This is because plastic does not biodegrade but simply breaks down into smaller and smaller pieces, which accumulate over time.

THE SOURCE

Most of the trash that makes up the Great Pacific Garbage Patch is not specifically dumped into the ocean. Approximately 80 percent of all marine debris is from land-based sources.[10] It is generated by littering or careless disposal of trash along shorelines and inland. Litter can make its way into storm drains, which then carry the debris into waterways and out to sea by currents. Tsunami debris likewise contributes to garbage in the ocean. The 2011 Japanese tsunami swept tens of thousands of pounds of material into the water.

Marine debris is also derived from ocean-based sources, including boats, offshore oil rigs, and ships. Of the ocean-based debris, much of it is in the form of discarded fishing nets and lines. Cargo ships have been known to lose containers at sea

Annually, only approximately 10 percent of plastics are recycled. The rest end up in places such as landfills and oceans.

Enormous amounts of cargo travel on the sea every day aboard gargantuan ships.

and contribute a range of garbage to the ocean, including toys, tennis shoes, and sports equipment.

It would be nearly impossible to simply scoop up all the trash in the ocean because of the sheer volume of debris and the fact that it is always moving. Additionally, there is no means to remove the smaller debris without also removing marine plankton from the ocean, which are vital to the ecosystem. The debris is even found on the seafloor. Since nonprofit organizations and scientists alike have further studied the size and impacts of the Great Pacific Garbage Patch and other ocean regions over recent decades, marine debris has garnered a growing audience. The effects of marine debris on habitats, fish, wildlife, humans, and Earth have become a global concern.

Marine debris from North America takes approximately six years to get to the Great Pacific Garbage Patch. It takes approximately one year for trash from Japan and other Asian countries to reach the patch.

TSUNAMI DEBRIS

In March 2011, a devastating tsunami struck Japan following a powerful earthquake in the Pacific Ocean. In the receding waters, the wreckage of people's homes and lives was washed out to sea. Since then, scientists and researchers have monitored and tracked the tsunami debris in an attempt to better understand what happens to plastics in the ocean, including how they move, how fast they break down, and their effect on marine species. The tsunami is of particular interest to scientists because they know the specific date the debris entered the ocean and where it entered. This helps them understand where debris travels and how quickly it moves.

Chapter

TWO

A SHORT HISTORY OF TRASH

Throughout time, people have dealt with waste in many different ways. In early civilizations, humans reused or repurposed whatever they could. Food waste was often fed to livestock or used for compost. Other trash was buried or burned. In ancient Rome, when populations rose and the amount of waste increased, the Romans established one of the first waste management systems. Not only did they build

Researchers have found everything from food wrappers to bed mattresses in garbage patches.

Between 20 million and 50 million people died of the plague during the Middle Ages.

a sewer system, but they also had garbage collectors. These people collected refuse from the streets and dumped it in a pit outside the city. But this system was not maintained after the fall of Rome, and the plagues that swept across Europe during the Middle Ages were a testament to the lack of sanitary waste management. Cities became more populated over time, and residents created more trash and left it to rot in the streets. This led to the spread of diseases and caused countless deaths. Eventually, fledgling waste management systems attempted to stem the tide of disease. One of the prevailing disposal methods was to dump trash into rivers or waterways.

The Age of Sanitation began in the mid-1800s. It included municipal waste collection and disposal in an effort to improve human health. Cities were more sanitary than in the Middle Ages, but at the same time, populations continued growing. There was more trash than ever before, and it was disposed of in incinerators, landfills outside city limits, or in rivers and oceans. By 1975, all US states had solid-waste regulations, and recycling started to become a normal part of waste disposal. Still, not all waste was disposed of properly, and much of it ended up in waterways and oceans.

PLASTIC WASTE PRODUCERS

A 2015 study quantified the amount of trash that ends up in the ocean every year. It also identified the major sources of the debris. The study found that the country producing the greatest amount of marine trash was China. Indonesia was the second-highest contributor. The United States was number 20 on the list. The reason the United States made the top 20 is twofold. First, the United States has long coastlines with large population densities. The second factor that put the United States on that list is its consumerism and the related popularity of plastic, single-use products.

In the United States, 380 billion plastic bags and wraps are used every year.[2]

THROWAWAY LIVING

Following World War II, the civilian uses for plastic skyrocketed. By the 1950s, disposable plastic items, such as plastic cups, food trays, utensils, and wrappers, were all the rage. In fact, *Life* magazine's August 1955 issue celebrated "throwaway living."[3] The cover of the magazine pictured a man, woman, and child tossing disposable items into the air like party confetti. The idea of not having to clean up after a meal because you could simply dispose of used items revolutionized the world. At the time, the use of plastic, disposable items in the home was advertised as a way to save housewives hours of cleaning.

DISPOSABLE LIFESTYLE

Modern technology brought with it a whole new type of waste, including more mass-produced items and greater amounts of packaging. At the beginning of the 1900s, scientists found a way to heat and mold petroleum-based synthetic resin into any shape. There were many possible uses for this plastic. During World War II (1939–1945), scientists further studied how this new product could be used in place of raw materials that had become difficult to obtain during wartime because the materials were allocated for military use. Plastic production shot up from 10,000 short tons (9,000 metric tons) in 1927 to 325,000 short tons (295,000 metric tons) per year by 1943.[1] Yet just as plastic played a role in war, it took on a role in peacetime, too. It was heralded as a wonder product, forever changing the world, and it was soon used in just about every part of people's daily lives.

Today, plastic is pervasive—people drink from it, eat out of it, play with it, wear it, and use it in countless products. Micro plastics are even found in bath and beauty products, such as face washes and toothpastes. Additionally, many plastic items, such as water bottles, straws, and bags, are tossed in the

The average American uses 167 plastic water bottles each year and only recycles 38 of them.

garbage after one use. This era of disposable consumer culture has been called the Age of Plastic. As of 2014, 311 million tons (282 million metric tons) of plastic had been produced worldwide.[4] That number is expected to double by 2034. A particular concern with plastic is that it is the only product on Earth that will never biodegrade. Plastic is forever. That means all the molecules of plastic ever created still exist on the planet somewhere. As Moore put it, "Only we humans make waste that nature can't digest."[5]

This is especially troubling for plastic debris that makes its way into the oceans.

There are an estimated 5.25 trillion pieces of plastic in the oceans.[8]

The oceans have a remarkable ability to absorb pollutants, even oil from spills, but not plastic. Of the human trash that makes its way into the ocean, approximately 80 percent of it is plastic.[6] It amounts to approximately 8.8 million short tons (8 million metric tons) of plastic going into the ocean each year.[7] Some of it starts out small, such as nurdles. These preproduction plastic pellets are the basic ingredient for making other plastic items. Other debris that goes into the ocean begins as larger items. The items may break down over time in the sun and saltwater, but they do not biodegrade. They simply break down into smaller and smaller pieces, eventually becoming micro plastics.

Moore and his team collected all types of trash from the North Pacific Gyre.

That is exactly what Moore found when he began investigating the debris in the North Pacific. Moore took his boat, *Alguita*, and a small crew back to the North Pacific Gyre. One part of his study involved collecting water samples from various depths and locations of the garbage patch. He took the samples to the Sea Lab in Redondo Beach, California, where they were examined to determine the content and concentration of plastic. Every sample researchers looked at had plastic in it. In fact, studies of the Great Pacific Garbage Patch have shown there are 1.9 million bits of micro plastic per square mile (730,000 bits per sq km).[9] That is, if you had 1,000 one-liter bottles of water, three or four bottles would have a piece of plastic in them.

INDICATIONS OF A PROBLEM

Moore's encounter with the Great Pacific Garbage Patch and his unrelenting attempts to study the phenomenon were responsible for bringing the issue of ocean debris to the public's attention. Yet there had been indications of a growing problem in the world's oceans decades before. In the early 1970s, scientists warned about garbage making its way into the ocean. Two researchers from the Woods Hole Oceanographic Institution found pieces of debris littering the Sargasso Sea in the

North Atlantic Gyre. Other researchers discovered that Laysan albatross and other animals in the North Pacific were eating bits of plastic. One researcher kept a log of the junk she came across during a trip to study the North Pacific. At 600 miles (970 km) from the shoreline, she was alarmed at the amount of man-made debris in the ocean.

As people became more aware of the problem, they brought it to the attention of world leaders. As a result, various governments took some measures to stop or limit the amount of debris that entered the ocean. Then, between 1985 and 1988, the US National Oceanic and Atmospheric Administration (NOAA) began studying the distribution and characteristics of plastics in the North Pacific Ocean. They noted concentrations of debris in certain areas. Little did they understand the magnitude of the issue at that time, and that it would continue to worsen into the 2000s.

PLASTIC EVERYWHERE

Scientists have developed many kinds of plastic, each with a slightly different chemical construction. These plastics have different densities, such that some will float and others will sink in seawater. Different types of plastics are used to make different types of products. Here are a few examples:

PLASTIC	USE
Polyethylene terephthalate [PET/PETE]	soda bottles
Polyester [PES]	polyester clothing
Polyethylene [PE]	plastic bags
High-density polyethylene [HDPE]	detergent bottles
Polyvinyl chloride [PVC]	plumbing pipes
Polypropylene [PP]	drinking straws
Polyamide (nylon) [PA]	toothbrushes
Polystyrene [PS]	takeout food containers

POLYMER CHEMISTRY

At first, the term *plastic* meant any material that could be molded or shaped into something else. It referred to organic materials, such as clay, glass, and wood. Over time, the term has come to refer mostly to the synthetic material made by harvesting hydrocarbons from petroleum.

The basic building blocks of modern plastics are monomers, single molecules that can be bonded to other identical molecules. Chemists harvest monomers from petroleum and combine them in different ways to form polymers, or large chains of molecules. Arrangements of polymers are the basis for all kinds of durable plastics that can be made into items of different shapes, sizes, and colors.

Plastics are often made into small pellets called nurdles. This raw form of plastic is easily shipped to manufacturers that use the nurdles to make different types of plastic products, such as shoes, toys, car bumpers, and more.

Nurdles are used to create all types of plastic products, including containers.

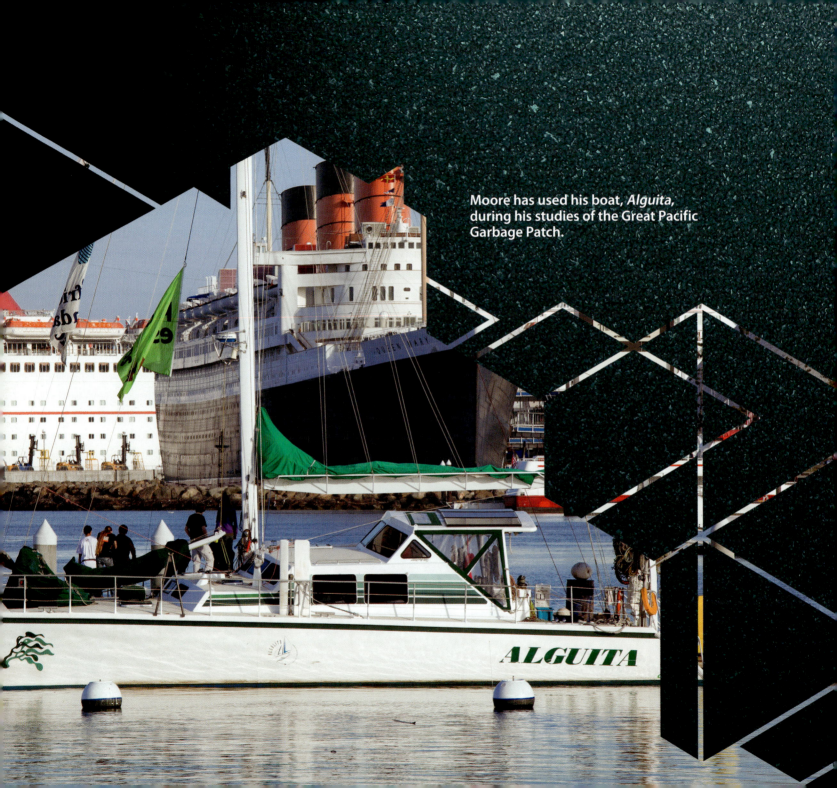

Moore has used his boat, *Alguita*, during his studies of the Great Pacific Garbage Patch.

THREE

IMPACT ON MARINE HABITATS

T he ocean is littered with debris, not just on the surface but throughout its depths. As much as 70 percent of all marine debris sinks, blanketing the ocean floor with trash.[1] In addition, coral reefs and coastlines are increasingly harmed by the growing amount of marine debris.

OCEAN HABITAT

Although the issue of marine debris was studied before Moore first sailed through the garbage patch in 1997, he was so affected by what he had seen that he wanted

CAPTAIN MOORE AND ALGALITA

In 1994, before his discovery of the Great Pacific Garbage Patch, Moore founded Algalita. This organization is dedicated to restoring kelp forests and improving the quality of water along California's coastline. Moore was already concerned about the existence of trash in water. So when he came across the garbage patch in the Pacific Ocean, Moore was outraged by it, especially since it was so far from any populated areas. "Plastic garbage does not belong in the ocean any more than sharks belong in municipal swimming pools," he said.[4] As a result, Moore redirected Algalita's focus to bringing attention to the amount of debris in the world's oceans. The organization also studies the impact of marine debris on oceans.

to study it further. From aboard *Alguita*, Moore and his crew trawled the ocean, gathering a great deal of trash in all shapes and sizes. The larger pieces of garbage included jumbo plastic jars, soda bottles, nets, toothbrushes, crates, and more. There were smaller pieces of trash and countless micro plastics, too. Among the micro plastics Moore found were small, seemingly harmless preproduction plastic pellets. Of the billions of pounds of nurdles manufactured every year, many are spilled on-site at factories and end up in the ocean. They are some of the most common types of marine debris. Moore also sampled the Los Angeles and San Gabriel Rivers, which empty into the Pacific Ocean, and estimated that 236 million nurdles washed into the ocean there every three days.[2]

During another study, Moore's crew collected 27,484 micro plastics from an area 80 miles (130 km) long by 3 feet (1 m) wide. This is equal to 2.7 pounds (1.2 kg) of plastic particles per square mile.[3]

Perhaps most telling of the degree of pollution in the North Pacific were the samples of seawater Moore examined for their plankton count. Plankton are the anchors of the marine food chain, but in initial samples collected by Moore and his team, they were overwhelmed by plastic bits. By weight, the micro plastic particles outweighed the plankton six to one.

Moore found plastics and other debris during his studies of
the garbage patch.

LAUNDRY LINT

Laundry lint is the fluffy mat of gray matter usually found in clothes dryers. Yet much of it comes off clothes in the washer, making its way past treatment systems and into the ocean. One fleece jacket, for example, can shed 2,000 polyester fibers in a single wash. As a result, these microscopic plastic fibers contribute to marine debris. A team of scientists combed 18 beaches around the world and found synthetic lint at every one of those beaches. While the direct impact of the synthetic laundry lint on the marine environment was unknown, the study showed yet another method for plastics to make their way into the ocean.

Other subsequent samples found the ratio of plastic to plankton by weight in some areas of the gyre was ten to one. That translated into an ocean filled with ten times more plastic than food for marine wildlife. Other scientists dispute this claim, however, saying Moore's samples and methods were flawed. Moore used the dry weights of both plankton and plastic for his calculations, but plankton are mostly water when they are alive, so this underestimates the plankton. In addition, his samples included large pieces of plastic debris, which are rare. Plankton populations also vary widely from season to season. Multiple data points would yield more accurate results, but Moore's samples were taken within a week of each other. Other studies have found that there are significantly more plankton in the ocean than there is plastic.

Not only are pellets and plastic debris clogging the oceans, but they are also made from a variety of different chemicals that give them the versatility they offer. What's more, nurdles and other plastics attract, absorb, and concentrate toxic chemicals and pollutants. The persistent organic pollutants (POPs) that nurdles and other plastics attract are a good measure of the pollution in oceans. In one recent study to understand the distribution of pollutants in plastic marine debris, volunteers in 23 countries around the world each collected 100 to 200 nurdles from coastal locations and wrapped them in paper or tinfoil. The volunteers noted the location of the samples, which were then tested for their levels of organic pollutants. The results found that the world's oceans were essentially a toxic soup, and that oceans near developed or industrial areas were the most polluted with POPs. Plastic collected from the Great Pacific Garbage Patch was no exception.

CORAL REEFS

Coral reefs are sometimes called the "rainforests of the sea."[5] The corals themselves are actually animals, not plants, and together they form reefs, which are critical ecosystems for the ocean and for Earth. Healthy coral reefs are among the most biologically diverse ecosystems on the planet. Many types of marine life depend on reefs, from the smallest algae to the largest sharks. Furthermore, reefs provide coastal protection from storms or erosion. But marine debris damages these fragile ecosystems.

Fishing nets, for example, can get caught on coral reefs as they roll through the ocean, ripping off coral heads. As the

Americans use 3 million plastic water bottles every hour.[6]

GHOST NETS

Among all marine debris, one of the greatest issues is derelict fishing nets, also known as ghost nets. In the past, fishing nets and lines were made of organic materials, such as wool or silk, that would biodegrade over time. Today, however, most nets are made of synthetic materials, which never break down. When abandoned in the ocean, they take on a life of their own. The nets tangle together; ensnare marine life, coral, and other debris; and tumble through the ocean. They have become such a problem that NOAA has created the GhostNet Detection Project to locate and remove the nets.

Debris such as plastic bags can cause irreparable damage to coral reefs.

nets move with ocean currents, they gather mass and weight, making them even more destructive as they crush and damage the coral they roll over. In addition to derelict fishing nets, other debris that collects in the ocean can smother coral reefs. It damages the coral and impedes growth, sometimes even killing the coral. Even small items play a role in degrading the overall reef habitat, and scientists are beginning to study the effects of micro plastics. Researchers from the Australian Research Council Centre of Excellence for Coral

Reef Studies have discovered that coral will eat micro plastics. These indigestible plastics can have negative effects on coral. Research to understand this aspect of the marine debris issue on reefs as a whole is ongoing.

While marine debris is just one of the factors contributing to the destruction of coral reefs in the Pacific and around the world, it has become an issue of growing concern. Along with marine debris, general pollution, overfishing, and global climate change are causing the reefs to die. As of 2016, 20 percent of coral reefs had already been destroyed, and of the remaining reefs, 25 percent were in immediate peril.[7]

BEACHES

Curtis Ebbesmeyer, an oceanographer who studies currents and marine debris, is intimately familiar with the garbage patches

Curtis Ebbesmeyer has studied marine debris extensively.

More than 90 percent of all life on the planet is found in the ocean.[9]

in the Pacific Ocean. He is an expert in understanding how currents move and what happens when swirls of marine debris travel toward the shoreline. "When it gets close to an island, the garbage patch barfs, and you get a beach covered with this confetti of plastic," he explained.[8]

Some of the beaches most directly affected by the Great Pacific Garbage Patch are on Hawaii and Midway Atoll. This string of islands in the Pacific Ocean acts like a comb as currents pass through them, snagging large amounts of marine debris. Beaches that were once idyllic and pristine are now fouled with trash from the ocean. Midway Atoll is located in the North Pacific, about halfway between Asia and North America. It is home to diverse marine wildlife. Historically, its beaches were soft, powdery white sand. Now, tens of thousands of pounds of marine debris wash onto the shores every year, littering the sand. The US Fish and Wildlife Service as well as dedicated volunteers attempt to clean it up regularly, but as soon as one removal effort ends, another must begin.

KAMILO BEACH, HAWAII

Long before the invention and mass production of plastic, indigenous Hawaiians understood that the ocean currents brought items to shore from faraway places. On Kamilo Beach at the southernmost tip of the Big Island of Hawaii, indigenous people would look for large logs that had drifted in from the Pacific Northwest. They used the logs to build dugout canoes. While driftwood still washes ashore at Kamilo Beach, it is far outnumbered by trash—so much so that the area is now referred to as Trash Beach.

Among the debris on the shore are discarded laundry baskets, basketballs, bottles, buoys, nets, bottle caps, tubs, tires, and tons and tons of micro plastic chips. The beach is literally a trash dump. The presence of such a large amount of trash both degrades the coastal ecosystem and causes harm to species living there. The sand is not just covered in debris, but also intermingled with plastic. On some beaches, researchers have found that sand is no longer made only of crushed rock but also of small broken-down plastic pieces. In these places, a handful of beach sand reveals as much micro plastic as actual sand.

Healthy ocean habitats are needed for healthy fish and wildlife. Yet as the oceans continue to collect debris, as in the Great Pacific Garbage Patch, the entire food web is at risk through both direct and indirect impacts that threaten biodiversity.

PLASTIGLOMERATES

As a result of the amount of plastic debris accumulating on beaches, scientists have found plastic rocks. These plastiglomerates are created when plastic debris mixes with rock, sand, shells, or coral at high temperatures. The scientists speculate that the rocks have formed as a result of fires or lava flows. With the heat, the plastic melts and fuses organic material together. In cases where coral or rock are porous, the plastic seeps into the pores. Sometimes, the plastic doesn't melt completely and is still recognizable as its original form, such as a toothbrush or plastic utensil.

PHOTOSYNTHESIS IN THE OCEAN

Phytoplankton are microscopic one-celled plants, and despite their size, they play an enormous role in sequestering carbon from the atmosphere. In fact, marine photosynthesis makes life on land possible by producing oxygen. Just like land plants, phytoplankton need carbon dioxide, water, and energy from the sun. They use these to produce their food. Oxygen is a by-product of the photosynthesis process and is released into the surrounding seawater and into the air.

While the majority of photosynthesis in the ocean takes place near the surface, it also occurs to a depth of approximately 650 feet (200 m). If large enough concentrations of micro plastics are found in the ocean, they could have the potential to inhibit photosynthesis, as they would block sunlight. This would have implications for the entire marine food web, since phytoplankton provide food for other consumers in the marine food web.

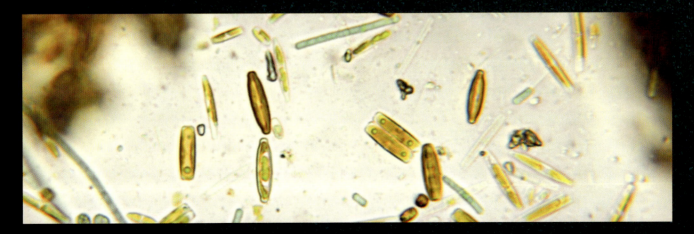

Diatoms are a type of phytoplankton.

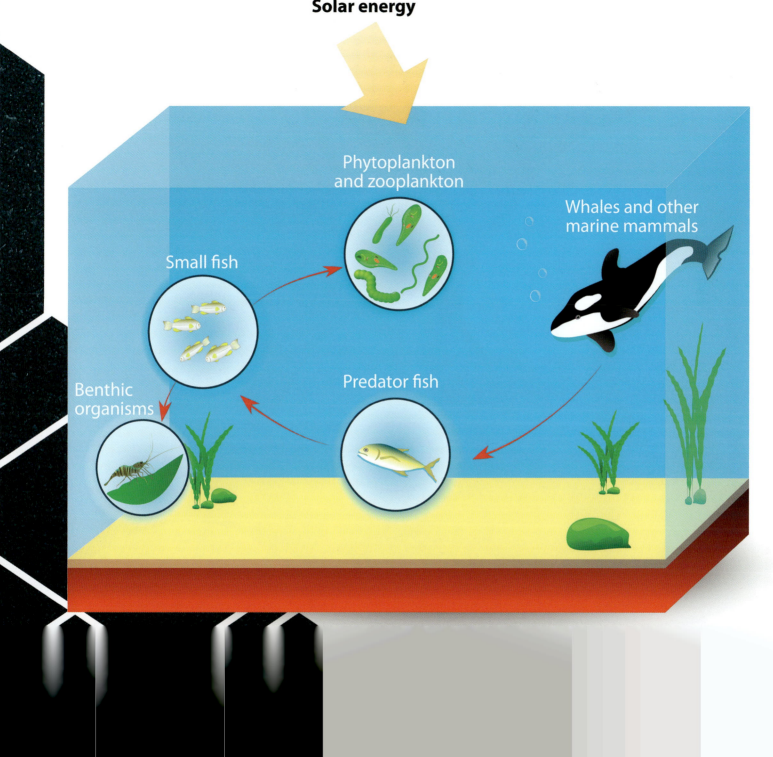

Solar energy

Phytoplankton and zooplankton

Whales and other marine mammals

Small fish

Predator fish

Benthic organisms

Chapter
FOUR

IMPACT ON FISH AND WILDLIFE

Species from the smallest single-celled organism to the largest whale need healthy ecosystems in order to thrive. And with the growing amount of marine debris degrading these ecosystems, scientists studying the Great Pacific Garbage Patch are finding the number of sea creatures killed or harmed every year is in the millions.

Ocean predators mistake plastic bags for jellyfish and eat them. Jellyfish themselves also eat micro plastic.

ONE INSECT IS THRIVING

While many species are affected by the Great Pacific Garbage Patch and marine debris around the world, not all species are negatively impacted. Traditionally, insects called *Halobates sericeus*, or oceanic water striders, lay their eggs on organic material in the ocean. As the ocean becomes increasingly littered with inorganic material, the insect is taking advantage. Scientists are finding the insects are not particular about their nurseries and are laying eggs on plastic debris. A study revealed an increase in the number of water strider eggs that correlated with the increase in marine debris. There is concern, though, that while this species may be thriving, the increase in its population may upset the entire marine ecosystem.

MARINE LIFE

Plankton are the smallest plant and animal life in marine ecosystems. They include single-celled algae, krill, and jellyfish. They are the foundation of the marine food web. Yet zooplankton aren't always picky about what they eat and will ingest small items, including plastics. Studies that show heavy concentrations of plastic in the ocean suggest the potential for plastic debris to be ingested is quite high. As Moore described it, "If surface waters of the ocean are a sort of buffet, then the main course, even for the smallest creatures, could well be plastic bits that are as much a part of their lives as plastic stuff is in ours."[1]

Graduate students from the Scripps Institution of Oceanography at the University of California, San Diego studied marine life in the Great Pacific Garbage Patch. They wanted to better understand the magnitude of the problem. During their study in the North Pacific Gyre, they found that close to 9.2 percent of the fish in the gyre had evidence of plastic waste in their stomachs.[2] Their calculations indicated that fish in the gyre consume 12,000 to 24,000 short tons (11,000 to 22,000 metric tons) of plastic every year.[3] In an earlier

Most species of sea turtles are endangered.

study by the Algalita Foundation, 83 pieces of plastic were found in the stomach of one 2.5-inch (6.4 cm) lantern fish.[4] The bits of plastic can move throughout the food web as fish eat the micro plastics or zooplankton. Those fish then become meals for even larger fish. In this way, marine animals have become plastivores.

Fish are but one type of sea creature affected by marine debris. A 2012 study published by the United Nations Convention on Biological Diversity indicated that more than 600 marine species, from plankton to whales, are affected by plastic waste in ocean habitats.[5] Sea turtles are among those at risk, both from ingestion and entanglement. Oftentimes, turtles become ensnared in ghost nets or other debris. Those that cannot continue to swim are unable to hunt for food, and they starve. Others have the debris permanently caught around them, impeding proper growth. Still others mistake plastic bags, a type of marine debris, for jellyfish, which are the turtles' main food source. Seals, dolphins, and other marine life also get tangled in marine debris, which can cause them to suffocate or drown. In other cases, debris caught around marine creatures can cause open wounds as they move and grow, which can ultimately get infected.

BIRDS

Seabirds are affected by marine debris as well, and many have become plastivores as they mistake trash for food. The Laysan albatross has become a symbol of the growing issue of

The Laysan albatross is not considered endangered, but there is little data about its population.

Each year, as many as 100,000 marine mammals and sea turtles and 1 million seabirds die from eating plastic.[8]

WORLD WAR II DEBRIS

The use of plastic materials was very much a part of the wartime effort in World War II. And since plastic does not biodegrade, the plastic produced and used during that time is still on the planet. In 2005, a bit of history revealed itself in the stomach of an albatross. The plastic found inside the dead bird had a serial number on it. A trace of the number indicated it had been part of a World War II seaplane that was shot down in 1944. Computer models showed the plastic piece had most likely spent ten years in the Western Garbage Patch of the Great Pacific Garbage Patch. It then spent another 50 years spinning in the Eastern Garbage Patch before it was snatched up by the bird.

garbage in the oceans, particularly the issue of plastic garbage. Midway Atoll in the Pacific is the nesting ground for 71 percent of all Laysan albatross, approximately 1 million birds.[7] But on an island surrounded by and laden with trash that has been washed ashore from the Great Pacific Garbage Patch, the ingestion rate of plastic by these birds is very high. Even more startling is that these birds feed the plastic to their young, and thousands of albatross chicks die every year with their guts full of plastic debris. The adult birds fish and forage for food, and they think the plastic bits are a natural food source. When they ingest plastic or feed it to their young, there is the potential for choking. With their stomachs packed full of plastic, there isn't enough room for real food. The birds are substituting plastic for nutrition and end up malnourished or starving to death.

On Midway Atoll, the carcasses of dead albatross are telling. The birds have two stomachs: one stores food to regurgitate for their young, and the other digests food for themselves. Studies of the dead birds show both stomachs are filled with plastic trash, such as bottle caps and lighters. The carcasses of the birds in various states of decomposition similarly reveal the pervasive nature of plastic. While the organic material of feathers and bones begins to return to the earth, at the birds' core are small heaps of plastic that have not decayed at all. In fact, the pieces of plastic are still intact and as recognizable as the day they left the factory.

It is not just the albatross that makes a meal of marine debris—many seabirds are at risk. Marine ecologists at the Commonwealth Scientific and Industrial Research Organisation in Australia studied the global, growing problem. They found that at least 80 species of seabirds consumed plastic, including gulls, penguins, and petrels. They expected this number to increase and predicted that by the year 2050 almost 100 percent of seabirds would consume meals of plastic.[9]

TOXINS

Ingestion of and entanglement in plastic marine debris can cause clear harm to marine life. Yet one aspect of ingestion that researchers are still trying to understand is the impact the toxins carried in plastics have on the species that ingest them. They want to know whether the toxins leach into the tissues of fish and other wildlife and what effects these toxins might have. One study of oysters, which are known to take in micro plastics, found that ingesting plastics impacts the oysters' reproductive system. Not only did the exposure reduce fertility, but there were

MARINE DEBRIS ACT
With the amount of ocean debris growing, and increasing awareness about it, the problem was brought before the US Congress. In 2006, Congress signed into law the Marine Debris Research, Prevention, and Reduction Act. The act launched NOAA's Marine Debris Program with the mission to "identify, determine sources of, assess, prevent, reduce, and remove marine debris and address the adverse impacts of marine debris on the economy of the United States, marine environment, and navigation safety."[10] In 2016, the Marine Debris Program celebrated ten years of successful efforts to address the marine debris issue.

also fewer offspring, and the offspring tended to be small.

A study published in 2013 that was conducted by Chelsea Rochman, a PhD student at San Diego State University, discovered liver stress in small fish as a result of toxins transferring into their systems from ingested plastic. This finding is troubling because of its implications for the rest of the food web. Rochman explained, "If these small fish are eating the plastic directly and getting exposed to these chemicals, and then a bigger fish comes up and eats five of them, they're getting five times the dose, and then the next fish—say, a tuna—eats five of those and they have twenty-five times the dose."[11] Scientists acknowledge that the

"It is impossible to quantify death in the ocean [because] weak and dying creatures are so rapidly consumed."[12]

—Captain Charles Moore

Predatory fish eat other fish, taking in chemicals from the plastics the prey fish may have eaten.

MANTA TRAWL

Many researchers studying the plastic problem at the Great Pacific Garbage Patch use a device called a manta trawl to collect samples from the ocean. The base of the device was modeled after the shape of a manta ray, the largest type of ray. The manta trawl has a wide opening, similar to a manta ray's mouth, and an extremely fine mesh net to collect microscopic objects above 0.013 inch (0.33 mm) in size. It also has two wings that keep it floating on the ocean's surface as the trawl is dragged behind a boat. The samples it collects are labeled and stored, along with information about where they were collected, the time of day they were collected, and other relevant details.

biomagnification of toxins as a result of plastic marine debris needs more research.

Regardless of the long-term impact of plastics and related toxins, hundreds of marine species are affected by the Great Pacific Garbage Patch. And while there is research still to be done, as Richard Thompson, a marine biologist at Plymouth University, put it, "It's hard to imagine that the [findings] are going to be positive."[13]

Ducks often mistake trash for food, which can cause stomach or bowel obstructions.

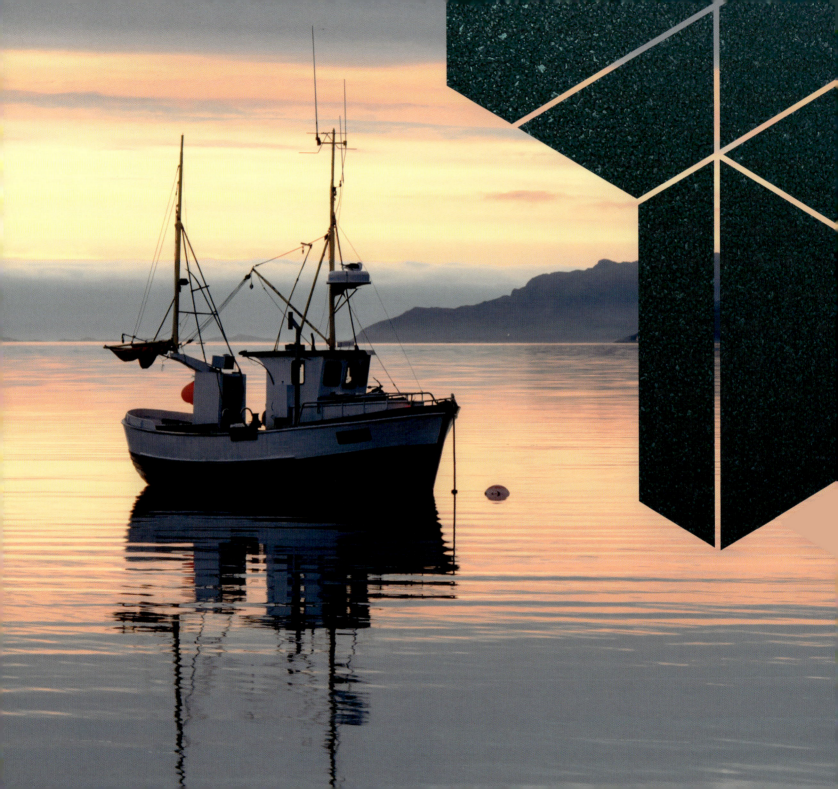

Chapter

FIVE

IMPACT OF MARINE DEBRIS ON HUMANS

As researchers continue to collect information about the impacts of marine debris on ecosystems and on marine fish and wildlife, they are similarly concerned about the impact the Great Pacific Garbage Patch has on humans economically, physically, and emotionally.

Fishers try to keep to clear waters so their boats are not damaged by debris.

In 2014, as part of the Good Mate program, 3,849 boaters traversed 416 miles (670 km) of waterways and collected 82,867 pounds (37,588 kg) of trash.[1]

GREEN BOATING

Boaters of all kinds know and understand the direct impact marine debris can have. They can also be part of the solution. The Ocean Conservancy created the Good Mate program in an effort to bring awareness to the role boaters can play in both preventing and cleaning up marine debris. The program offers tips and steps that boaters can take. These include having boaters take part in cleanup efforts, act as stewards of the ocean by taking measures to stop debris from entering the ocean, and spread the word to others. The hope is that if boat operators do their part, it will have a large impact on the amount of marine debris in the ocean.

ECONOMIC IMPACTS

As the Great Pacific Garbage Patch continues growing and ocean waste in general keeps accumulating, the effects are increasingly being felt economically. For boaters, large pieces of marine debris pose navigational hazards and can damage their vessels. Much of the damage to boats is the result of derelict fishing gear that gains mass as it rolls through the ocean. It can become tangled on boat propellers, eventually burning out an engine and docking a boat. When a boat is docked, there is a direct economic loss to the boat owner or business, who has to pay to have the boat repaired. There are further losses to those who depend on their boats to generate income. Commercial and recreational fishers are further affected by marine debris because it drives down fish populations. When there are fewer fish available, there is a loss of income for fishers.

Coastal areas depend on tourist dollars to support their economy. They lose revenue when debris reduces the beauty and recreational value of the shoreline. The beaches of the West Coast of the United States, Hawaii, Japan, and other places near the Great Pacific Garbage Patch are affected by debris that is both unsightly and unhealthy. In severe cases, beaches are even closed due to the amount of debris. In the water, the debris is a hazard to swimmers and divers who can become entangled in plastics or cut by sharp objects. In order to combat the problem of marine debris on beaches, many coastal cities have launched massive cleanup efforts, but these, too, come at a cost. In 2012, the Environmental Protection Agency (EPA) reported that US West Coast communities spend in excess of $520 million each year to keep beaches clean.[2]

PLASTIC FOR DINNER

Even more troubling than the growing economic cost of marine debris is the potential cost to human health. With more marine animals becoming plastivores, there is growing concern about what this means for humans at the top of the food chain. When humans eat fish that have ingested plastic, or have eaten other fish that have eaten plastic, the chain of events puts people at risk of dinner plates full of plastic and the toxins concentrated in them.

The chemicals and additives used to make plastic have proven negative effects on humans. These effects include increased risk of breast cancer in women, early puberty in girls, and endocrine disruption that may adversely affect developmental, reproductive,

NETS TO ENERGY

Generally, when derelict fishing nets are recovered, they are taken to a landfill. In Hawaii, though, there is a unique program to turn the abandoned gear into usable energy. Starting in 2002, nets are transported to a scrap metal recycling facility in Hawaii, where they are chopped into pieces. The pieces are then taken to a facility that creates energy from waste. There, they are burned. The steam produced by burning the nets drives a turbine, thus creating energy.

Any toxins fish consume may also be eaten by humans.

neurological, and immune systems. The US Department of Health and Human Services also reported that ingesting chemicals commonly found in plastic can cause joint pain, fatigue, weakness, skin anomalies, and loss of appetite.

Studies have shown that harmful chemicals are present in the seafood sold for human consumption. A 2015 study of fish sold in Californian markets revealed that 25 percent of them had some type of plastic debris in their digestive tract.[3] Humans don't usually eat the micro plastic debris itself but rather are at risk due to toxins that potentially collect in the tissues of the fish.

Those who rely on seafood as their primary source of protein, such as the Inuit in the North American Arctic, are especially at risk for exposure to harmful toxins. Studies of the Inuit peoples have found high levels of contaminants in their bodies. Researcher Theo Colborn said, "The Inuit diet of 'country food' which includes marine mammals such as beluga whale, narwhal and seal, puts them at the top of a contaminated food chain."[4] Colborn's study found the level of POPs in many Inuit exceeded Canada's "level of concern."[5] Other studies of Inuit had similar results, showing levels

"While current research cannot quantify the amount, plastic in the ocean does appear to contribute to [persistent, bioaccumulative, and toxic substances] in the human diet."[6]
—*Richard Engler, EPA chemist, 2012*

PLASTIC PRODUCTION

Despite risks to human health and the environment, plastic production worldwide continues to increase, as it has for more than 50 years. In 2013, 299 million tons (271 million metric tons) of plastic were produced, which was up 4 percent from the previous year. The average person in North America or Europe uses approximately 220 pounds (100 kg) of plastic each year, mostly in the form of packaging. People in Asia use an average of 44 pounds (20 kg) of plastic each year.[7]

The Inuit rely on fish as part of their diet.

of contaminants at much higher concentrations in Arctic communities than in people living in southern Canada.

A direct link between plastic marine debris and human health has yet to be established due to the difficulty in figuring out where people may have been exposed to certain toxins. Studies focus on three key areas. First, scientists want to know the extent to which plastics transfer toxins to organisms after the plastics are eaten. Next, they want to learn the extent to which micro plastics contribute to overall contamination exposure through the ocean, sediment, and food. Researchers also want to know what percentage of human exposure to pollutants occurs through seafood. The scientific community is divided about whether eating seafood contaminated with ocean plastic poses risks to human health. Yet scientists agree more research needs to be done.

MICROBEADS BANNED

At one time, many personal health care products, such as toothpaste and body washes, were manufactured with microbeads. The microbeads acted as abrasives, polishing skin and teeth surfaces. The microbeads do not break down. Oftentimes, they made their way into watersheds and the ocean. Due to growing concern over the effects of these beads on marine environments, individual US states took action to ban them from use. Illinois was the first. The state banned the production and sale of products containing the microbeads in 2014. Then in December 2015, President Barack Obama signed a bill that prohibited companies from manufacturing products containing plastic microbeads. By July 1, 2017, products containing microbeads could no longer be sold in the United States.

SIX

MONITORING AND CLEANUP EFFORTS

G iven the size of the Great Pacific Garbage Patch, the concentration of marine debris in it, and its location, the prospect of cleaning up the patch seems daunting, if not impossible. All cleanup efforts must be done with as little harm to marine life as possible. Yet scientists, students, and researchers are not giving up hope. They have come up with

Boyan Slat is one innovator who is coming up with possible solutions to ocean cleanup problems.

innovative ideas to put technology to work to rid the North Pacific Gyre, and Earth's other gyres, of garbage.

CLEANING IT UP

One idea that has garnered a great deal of attention, beginning in 2012, was from Dutch teenager Boyan Slat. He became aware of the Great Pacific Garbage Patch and marine debris in oceans around the world and was profoundly affected. So he pondered the feasibility of cleaning it up. Despite the naysayers who said it couldn't be done, Slat persevered. He began with research to estimate the size of the problem and how much plastic was in the top layers of the gyres. With the help of scientists in different parts of the world, Slat determined that by the year 2020 there would be 7.25 million tons (6.58 million metric tons) of plastic that could be extracted from the Great Pacific Garbage Patch.[1]

Conventional debris-removal efforts involve ships that fish for trash using nets. This activity uses a large amount of fuel and comes at a great economic cost. Slat, however, came up with an idea that would use the ocean's natural currents to move the garbage. As Slat said, "Why move through the ocean, when the ocean can move through you?"[2] Slat developed a

BOYAN SLAT

Boyan Slat, founder of the Ocean Cleanup, was still a teenager when he had the idea for the system that may one day clean up the Great Pacific Garbage Patch and other ocean areas like it. Growing up an avid ocean diver, Slat had taken notice of the marine debris where he swam and saw plastic bits on the beaches. On one particular diving trip to Greece, Slat's friend joked about all the jellyfish they'd seen. But they hadn't seen any jellyfish—just plastic bags. Soon after, for a school project, Slat was given the choice to research anything he wanted. He chose plastic marine debris and began actively researching the amount of debris in the ocean. From there, he continued exploring the ocean debris issue and founded the Ocean Cleanup.

Slat posed with a model of a barrier at an event in Scheveningen harbor, the Netherlands, in June 2016.

device called an array, shaped like a manta ray, to collect marine debris. His idea includes stretching long floating barriers between multiple arrays to catch debris as the ocean's currents move past them. The barriers are solid and extend a few feet deep into the ocean. The system acts like a simulated coastline, passively concentrating the plastic and moving it toward the array. Yet it allows for marine life to pass under the barriers instead of getting caught along with the debris. Slat concluded he could

"If we want to do something different, shouldn't we also have to think differently?"[3]

—Boyan Slat, founder of the Ocean Cleanup

The Ocean Cleanup may be able to remove as much as 50 percent of the trash in the Great Pacific Garbage Patch in 10 years.

sell the plastics collected by the array for recycling to US markets. The sales would more than cover expenses for the project.

In 2013, Slat founded the Ocean Cleanup, a Dutch nonprofit organization, to begin working in earnest toward cleaning up the Great Pacific Garbage Patch. With the help of numerous scientists, engineers, and advisers, the Ocean Cleanup developed a prototype of the array design and launched it in the North Sea, located between the United Kingdom and Scandinavia, in 2016. The system requires no additional energy to operate, as it is powered by ocean currents, and it can be scaled to any size. The goal of the Ocean Cleanup is to have a full deployment of the project in the Great Pacific Garbage Patch by 2020.

During the 2009 International Coastal Cleanup Day, 10 million pieces of trash were collected from ocean beaches. Of that amount, 1,126,774 pieces were plastic bags.[5]

Despite the Ocean Cleanup's best efforts to minimize impact on marine life, there are some potential drawbacks to the system. Some scientists are concerned that the Ocean Cleanup is not actually feasible. They note many potential issues with the system. For example, filtering methods like the one used by the Ocean Cleanup have no way to differentiate between plankton and plastics. As a result, many living things may be caught up in the process and never released back into the ocean.

Another technological innovation being developed to clean up marine debris includes a floating, solar-powered waterwheel designed to pull trash from the water, transfer it to a conveyor belt, and dump it in a large bin. Like Slat's array, the waterwheel uses no outside energy source. It is powered by the water around it, as well as solar energy. First launched in Baltimore Harbor in 2014, the wheel can clean up to 25.4 short tons (23 metric tons) of marine debris per day.[4] Another idea for cleaning up marine debris is an underwater skyscraper that collects plastic marine debris and generates clean hydroelectric power at the same time. It uses energy from the sun, the water, and the debris to move through the ocean to polluted areas.

In addition to technological advances to help clean up marine debris, there are hands-on cleanup efforts on beaches to help stem the tide of trash. One of the greatest global efforts, sponsored by the Ocean Conservancy, is International Coastal Cleanup Day. It calls for volunteers worldwide to scour beaches and waterways for trash that has been left behind by careless consumers or deposited on the shore by ocean currents. The effort in 2015 involved an estimated 800,000 volunteers who collected more than 18 million pounds (8 million kg) of trash.[6]

Experts predict there will be more plastic than fish in the oceans by 2050.

Another cleanup program includes NOAA's Marine Debris Program. In 2016, the group tackled debris on the northwestern Hawaiian Islands. On Midway Atoll National Wildlife Refuge, it collected

International Coastal Cleanup Day takes place in more than 90 countries around the world, including the Philippines.

67

GREAT PACIFIC GARBAGE PATCH GROWING

The Great Pacific Garbage Patch is both larger and denser than previously thought. Prior to launching cleanup arrays, the Ocean Cleanup embarked on the first-ever aerial surveillance of the garbage patch, which followed a mapping operation by a fleet of boats. In 2016, the group found that the core of the garbage patch spreads over approximately 386,000 square miles (1 million sq km) of the Pacific Ocean, yet may extend as far as 1,351,000 square miles (3.5 million sq km).[9] While other studies have garnered different results about the size and density of the patch, there is general consensus that the problem is growing.

15,206 pounds (6,897 kg) of marine debris in eight days.[7] It gathered the usual assortment of plastic pieces, bottle caps, bottles, and lighters, estimating at least half of the collection was from derelict fishing gear. NOAA has led this cleanup effort and others every year since 1996 and has recovered an estimated 5,500 short tons (5,000 metric tons) of marine debris.[8]

MONITORING AND TRACKING TOOLS

To better understand the size, content, and movement of the Great Pacific Garbage Patch, as well as how it changes over time, scientists are using technology to monitor and track the debris. NOAA's Marine Debris Program launched the Marine Debris Monitoring and Assessment Project. The information it collects about the types and amount of debris found both on land and at sea is entered into a database. The data can then be used to assess the progress of prevention programs and target resources and cleanup efforts to particular areas. The Marine Debris Program also has a Marine Debris Tracker app, as well as the GhostNet Detection Project. These NOAA projects incorporate computer modeling, satellite images, and GPS technology to track marine debris.

A NEW ERA OF PLASTICS

With growing concern about the pervasive nature of plastic and how much of it is used and disposed of every year, scientists have begun developing new types of plastic. Some are made from organic, plant-based materials, and others are made from petrochemicals. Different types of organic material used in some of these new plastics include corn, starch, sugarcane, and tapioca. The new plastics contain fewer fossil fuels, and use less of them for processing. Some of the plastics can be composted or recycled.

While these new biodegradable products are meant to be a sustainable alternative to traditional plastics, they do come with some flaws. The new plastics can break down, but to do so, they need to heat to certain temperatures that will not be met in the ocean. Also, these plastics will not float and will sink to the bottom of the ocean. They will not be exposed to the sun's rays, which could eventually break down the materials.

RECYCLING TECHNOLOGY

Recycling innovations for conventional plastics are on the rise. The American Chemistry Council (ACC) has a vested

THE NEW COCA-COLA BOTTLE

The Coca-Cola Company has a new product, but it isn't a beverage. It isn't even a food, although it is made from plants. It is the PlantBottle, a bottle made partially from plants in an effort to reduce plastic waste. The use of the bottle for products such as water, tea, and juice accounts for approximately 30 percent of the company's packaging in North America. This equals approximately 6 billion bottles per year. The product not only reduces greenhouse gas emissions in production, but it also saves millions of gallons of gasoline. The company's goal is to convert 100 percent of packaging to PlantBottles by the year 2020.[10]

Curbside recycling programs, available in many US communities, work to divert plastic out of the garbage.

interest in conventional plastic, as it represents leading manufacturers of plastic resin in the United States, including Dow Chemical, DuPont, and Exxon Mobil. It grants Innovation in Plastics Recycling awards to companies that "bring new technologies, products and initiatives to communities and the marketplace that demonstrate significant advancements in plastics recycling."[11] One award went to a company that recycled plastic into spray foam insulation. Another award went to Publix Super Markets, which streamlined its process for collecting rigid plastic packaging for recycling. Another organization, the Recycling Partnership, won the award for its work to increase curbside recycling efforts across the country through education and the provision of 115,000 large recycling carts.[12]

ANOTHER PERSPECTIVE

Much of the technology developed to clean up the Great Pacific Garbage Patch has focused on the patch itself rather than efforts to clean up shorelines. One team of researchers employed computer modeling to test whether this approach is most effective. Using simulations that took into account currents, the source of debris, and the amount of marine life both in the gyre and closer to land, the team determined that efforts closer to land would cut the amount of plastic in the ocean by 31 percent by 2025. The models indicated only a 17 percent decrease in the amount of plastic for cleanup efforts focusing on the gyre.[13]

Another new recycling innovation came from a team of chemists from the Shanghai Institute of Organic Chemistry and the University of California, Irvine. The team discovered a way to convert plastic waste into liquid fuel. The new method was developed based on the knowledge that plastic is made from oil or natural gas. The team looked at plastic not as waste but instead as a form of stored energy. The process uses less energy and makes a less-toxic product than previous methods used to break down plastics.

OCEAN CLEANUP ARRAY

The arrays to clean up the Great Pacific Garbage Patch developed by the Ocean Cleanup combine several simple yet effective engineering principles to catch marine debris. The first is that the system is completely passive, meaning the arrays don't move but wait for the ocean currents to bring debris to them. In this way, the ocean is doing the work of moving the debris, and the array acts like an artificial shoreline. Next, long booms extend outward from the array in a V-shape. They act like a funnel with the moving current, concentrating the debris at the array. The booms are flexible, so they bend rather than break in strong currents and storms. Nonpermeable screens hang 6.5 feet (2 m) below the booms, making it possible for marine life to pass underneath while still allowing for

debris collection. The array is responsible for ultimately collecting the debris and storing it until it can be recovered by ships and recycled.

The potential for the array to clean up debris in the ocean lies in its simplicity. If feasibility studies prove true, it will be both faster, more efficient, and cheaper than conventional cleanup methods. However, there is doubt in the scientific community about the array becoming a reality. To begin, while larger marine life may be able to move under the screens suspended from the booms, the effect on smaller marine life is still unclear, especially during the actual collection phase. Some people believe the array will interfere with navigation. There is also concern that the design underestimates the force of the ocean and its currents.

There are approximately 16,000 plastic manufacturing plants in the United States.

Chapter SEVEN

GARBAGE PATCH PREVENTION

Cleaning up the Great Pacific Garbage Patch and other garbage patches around the world is a major endeavor that is gaining increasing public awareness. Many people are optimistic about the possibility. But because 80 percent of the debris in the ocean originates on land, others believe the solution to the marine debris problem lies not in cleanup efforts but in stopping the debris before it reaches the water. People working for NOAA's Marine Debris Program believe prevention is the best solution, and efforts to solve the marine debris issue need to focus on reducing, reusing, and recycling.

40 DAYS AND 40 NIGHTS

Emily Smith of England lived without single-use plastic products for 40 days and 40 nights in an effort to bring awareness to the growing issue of plastic pollution and its impact on the oceans. Smith's biggest challenges included eating on the move, acquiring medicines, and finding trash can liners, because they all use plastic in some way. She hoped that her efforts would inspire others to make better choices about using single-use plastics and about recycling.

Each year, 8,800,000 short tons (8,000,000 metric tons) of debris enters the oceans from 192 countries.[2]

STOPPING IT AT THE SOURCE

Many groups fighting against marine debris call for cutting off plastic production at the source. However, one of the main reasons to keep producing plastics, especially single-use plastics, is economic. The top producers of plastic resin are represented by the ACC. The Society of Plastics Industries represents the numerous companies that manufacture plastic products using the approximately 150 billion pounds (68 billion kg) of resin made each year.[1] Both groups have a vested interest in maintaining and increasing plastic production. Behind automobile and steel production, plastics is the third-largest industry in the United States. And because the plastic industry is so large, it has both money and influence. As such, little concrete action has been taken by the industry to address the issue of marine debris or change production.

The power of the plastics industry is well illustrated by the fight against efforts to ban or tax the use of plastic bags. For example, California, which is on the front lines of Pacific Ocean debris, considered a statewide ban on plastic bags. Shoppers would have to bring or purchase a reusable tote or buy a four-to-six-cent paper bag to carry their purchases. The state

Approximately 100 billion plastic bags are used in the United States each year.

was met by incredible resistance and a historic lobbying effort by the plastics industry. Still, the ban was introduced in 2010 and was supported by environmentalists, shoppers, grocers, and retailers. Nonetheless, the ban failed to pass through the state senate. Politicians who opposed the bill claimed the ban on bags would create an undue burden for struggling families and send a message that the state "care[s] more about banning plastic bags than helping them put food on their table."[3] Yet the biggest opponent was the

ACC. To fight the bill, the group ran a massive campaign, including ads and radio spots, and also hired lobbyists. A spokesman for the ACC said the cost to already struggling families to purchase bags would be unfair. It also claimed there would be a loss of jobs in the plastics industry if demand for plastic bags dropped. The ACC promoted recycling as the solution to plastic trash.

BAG MONSTER

In an effort to raise awareness about the overuse of plastic bags in modern society, Andy Keller became the Bag Monster. He wore a costume that resembled a Yeti and was made out of 500 single-use plastic bags. The idea was to visually represent the number of bags the average person in the United States uses and discards every year. He also wanted to encourage consumers not to be bag monsters. Keller makes public appearances, lends out costumes, and has a blog to keep people informed about initiatives to ban plastic bags. Keller was sued by the top three plastic bag manufacturers. They claimed his efforts were harming their businesses. Two of the companies dropped the suit, and the third settled the case out of court.

But in 2014, the state legislature passed the bag ban law, and on September 30, 2015, California became the first state to ban all single-use plastic bags statewide. "We're the first to ban these bags, and we won't be the last," California governor Jerry Brown declared, adding that the ban would help "reduce the torrent of plastic polluting our beaches, parks and even the vast ocean itself."[4] Despite public support, the opposition rallied once again, led largely by the plastics industry, to stall the bag ban. Some estimates reported that an out-of-state company spent as much as $3 million to gather enough petition signatures to put the ban on hold and have it on the 2016 ballot.[5] On Election Day in November 2016, however, voters upheld the ban imposed by the state legislature, and California officially became the first state to ban the sale of single-use plastic bags at the checkout counter. However, plastic bags are still available for meat, bread, produce, bulk food, and perishable items.

POSITIVE PARTNERSHIPS

Due to growing public support, other positive changes are taking place to address the marine debris issue. The Global Partnership on Marine Litter (GPML) is an international initiative that brings together policy makers, governments, academics, conservationists, nongovernmental agencies, the private sector, and businesses to reduce and prevent marine debris. Launched in 2012, GPML's goals include reducing the impact of marine debris on habitats and wildlife, increasing awareness of the issue, improving international cooperation, and promoting research to understand the full impact of toxins related to plastics.

Another initiative to find solutions to the marine debris problem, the Declaration of the Global Plastics Associations for Solutions on Marine Litter, was announced in 2011 by a coalition of 47 plastics associations from around the world. The joint declaration was a commitment by these associations to take action. It resulted in measurable progress in six key areas, including education, research, public policy, best practices, plastics recycling and recovery, and plastic pellet containment. As of the end of 2015, a total of 65 associations from

"Waste is an antiquated concept. The only reason to throw anything away is because it's too difficult to reuse. We don't have to waste anything, we just have to start making things that are easy to reuse or recycle."[6]

—*Captain Charles Moore*

34 countries had signed the declaration, and leaders from worldwide plastics organizations announced that 260 projects were in progress or had been planned or completed.[7]

AMERICA RECYCLES DAY

The annual America Recycles Day on November 15 encourages people to learn about and take action to reduce waste and to recycle more. In 2015, President Barack Obama said, "Every American has a role to play in preserving our planet for future generations. . . . Today, we acknowledge the importance of reusing materials and reducing consumption, and we recognize that a recycling bin may often be a better alternative to a garbage can."[9] On America Recycles Day, people can pledge to recycle. They can host community events to inspire and educate people about recycling. In 2015, there were 1.5 million participants and 1,500 registered events across the country, including stalls at farmers' markets, poster contests for young students, and the Trashy Flashy Fashion Show in Tampa Bay, Florida, that showcased garments made from at least 75 percent recycled materials.[10]

Another tangible solution for preventing marine debris is to redouble recycling efforts. The current system is a linear approach, where single-use plastics are produced, consumed, and then disposed of. As of 2013, the EPA estimated that only 9 percent of the plastic in the United States was recycled.[8] Additionally, only a few types of plastics are actually recyclable. Instead, the system needs to close the loop—plastics need to be produced, consumed, and recycled so they can be used again. This curbs the demand for new plastic production, while keeping plastic from ending up as marine debris.

EDUCATION AND AWARENESS

Education and awareness will also keep the Great Pacific Garbage Patch and others from growing. A campaign to raise awareness was launched in June 2008 by Dr. Marcus Eriksen. JUNK is a sailboat designed out of 15,000 plastic bottles, old fishing nets, airplane parts, and repurposed sailboat masts. It left California for Hawaii, hoping to get people's attention about the need to change consumer use of plastics. It arrived

Joel Paschal, *right*, and Dr. Marcus Eriksen sailed from California to Hawaii aboard JUNK.

safely in Honolulu after 88 days at sea, sailing 2,600 miles (4,200 km).[11] Government agencies are also joining the effort. NOAA, in addition to being directly involved with research about and the cleanup of marine debris, focuses on prevention in the form of education, classroom curricula, community outreach, and events. For example, the group supports projects that raise awareness of marine debris and has produced a Trash Talk video series to address the issue. Each video in the series touches on a different aspect of the marine debris issue.

Only 5 to 10 percent of the plastics produced are recovered.[12]

There are many other individuals and organizations focused on raising awareness and educating the public as well. The Algalita Foundation has been instrumental in researching the Great Pacific Garbage Patch and its impacts on marine life. It has various education programs and believes that every individual has the power to be part of the marine debris solution.

People on the front lines of the marine debris problem understand that the Great Pacific Garbage Patch and others are growing, and the plastics industry is still producing plastic. Through education and awareness, people can make small changes that, combined with the efforts of other individuals, can make big differences. One way to start is by bringing

ART FROM GARBAGE

Since the issue of marine debris has worsened, some people are getting creative about how to bring awareness to the general public. One group of artists and scientists scoured the shores of remote beaches in Alaska. They found debris that had washed ashore and used it to create pieces of art for an exhibition. It opened in Alaska in 2014 before traveling the world. Other artists around the world are also creating marine debris art to call attention to the problem, and NOAA even sponsors a marine debris art contest every year.

a reusable bag to the store, whether for grocery shopping, clothes shopping, or getting takeout food. Carrying a reusable water bottle can also save millions of plastic bottles from becoming part of the plastic problem, as will carrying a reusable coffee mug or cup. When packing a lunch, avoid plastic bags and utensils. Instead, use containers and silverware that can be brought home, washed, and reused. Other ways to cut down on waste include avoiding straws and heavily packaged food and urging friends and family to do the same.

NO MORE BOTTLED WATER

One way to reduce the number of plastic bottles produced is to curb demand. Using reusable water bottles cuts down on the need for factories to make bottled water. Yet filling personal water bottles in traditional water fountains or public restroom sinks is often tricky because the bottles are too tall to fit under the tap. To solve the problem, many schools, universities, airports, and other locations have installed rapid water bottle filling stations. These stations are specifically designed to fill tall water bottles quickly with purified water. The goal is to make it easier for people to avoid buying bottled water.

Chapter
EIGHT

THE OCEANS' FUTURE IN THE AGE OF PLASTIC

The Great Pacific Garbage Patch, made up largely of plastic debris, is growing, and it is gaining attention. Scientists and researchers are investigating the effects of marine debris on the ocean habitat, fish and wildlife, and humans. The issue

Scientists do not know much about the long-term impact of marine debris on animals and the environment.

Recycling plastics is one way to keep them from forming garbage patches in oceans.

becomes how to move forward in an age of plastic.

THERE IS NO GARBAGE PATCH

Some researchers are concerned that inaccuracies or hype in the media may serve to undermine public efforts to reduce the flow of debris to the ocean. A researcher from Oregon State University, Angelicque "Angel" White, studied the debris in the North Pacific and concluded that the garbage patch is not a cohesive patch twice the size of Texas. White believes portrayals of a Texas-sized patch present a false concept of something that can easily be removed or cleaned up. Rather, the debris field in the surface ocean is diffuse and widespread. It is intermingled with a wide variety of marine plankton. It is more like Texas was broken into hundreds of millions of pieces and scattered in the North Pacific. This difference in presentation matters, because while removing an island of trash may seem possible, removing many small pieces from the middle of the ocean is much less feasible. It would come with great energy costs, as well as potentially devastating the plankton communities living on or around plastic. White states, "The more practical answer is to reduce the input of plastic into our oceans in the first place."[1] Moreover, White and others point out a bias in the often-repeated statement that the mass of plastic waste outweighs plankton. That study compared only the dry weight of plastic and plankton collected from nets with a wide mesh size of 0.013 inches (0.33 mm). Therefore, a significant fraction of planktonic mass smaller than that was missed. While White does not deny there is a growing problem with marine debris, she believes it is important for researchers and advocacy groups to not overstate their findings, in order to come to effective solutions.

Other experts agree that the concept of a physical patch or floating island of garbage is deceptive. They believe the real problem is micro debris. Aerial surveillance of the Great Pacific Garbage Patch in 2016 confirmed the lack of high concentrations of visible debris. Some scientists use this

It is estimated that 8 million pieces of marine debris enter oceans and seas every day.[2]

POPS INTERNATIONAL YOUTH SUMMIT

The goal of the annual POPs youth summit in California is to bring together youth ages 11 to 18 from around the world in an effort to solve the marine debris problem. To attend the summit, teams of two to four students must come up with an innovative idea, project, or solution relating to the issue of marine debris. The projects must focus on scientific research, waste reduction, legislative action, community outreach, or art. At the summit, students attend sessions with speakers who have expertise in marine debris. They also attend workshops, present their own projects, and network with others working toward marine debris solutions.

HISTORY OF THE PLASTIC BAG

The plastic bag that is so ubiquitous in modern society made its debut as a sandwich bag in 1957. Soon it was used in the dry cleaning industry. Bags for shoppers didn't emerge until the 1970s and were first found in retail stores such as Sears, Montgomery Ward, and J.C. Penney, and then in grocery stores, launching the great "paper or plastic?" debate. Yet despite the bags' growing popularity, the first plastic bag recycling program didn't begin until 1990.

lack of debris to discredit Moore's original assessment of the garbage patch back in 1997: "I was confronted, as far as the eye could see, with the sight of plastic . . . plastic debris was floating everywhere."[3] Since then, Moore has worked to more accurately define the marine debris issue in the North Pacific, yet misconceptions remain. Tamara Galloway of the University of Exeter echoes concerns about the misconceptions and points out that coastal areas are much more highly contaminated.

ANTHROPOCENE ERA

Due to the growing influence of humans on Earth, many scientists believe the planet has entered a new geologic time period, the Anthropocene Era. This claim arises from the fact that humans have forever altered Earth's geology. Humans have been the catalyst for mass extinction, have polluted Earth's ecosystems, and have impacted the planet irreversibly.

While humans have manipulated Earth's resources for millennia, it wasn't until the mid-1900s that the era of human influence truly began. Following World War II, there was a large population boom, greenhouse gas emissions increased,

Improper trash disposal can lead to pollution on beaches and in waterways.

> "The continued use of verbiage such as 'plastic islands,' 'twice the size of Texas,' is pure hyperbole that I personally believe undermines the credibility of those that should be focused on helping reduce the source stream of marine debris to our oceans."[5]
>
> —*Angel White, associate professor at Oregon State University, 2016*

and the current disposable consumer culture began. Plastics have greatly contributed to this Anthropocene Era.

A team of scientists from the University of Leicester studied the impact of plastic on the planet. "The geology of plastic is something I've been interested in simply because there's so much of it. Plastics are a mid-twentieth century invention and manufacturing has gone from nothing to something like 300 million tons a year. It's clearly escaping into the environment in various places," explained geologist team member Dr. Jan Zalasiewicz.[4] The study suggests Earth's

Scientists estimate there are more than 5 trillion pieces of trash in Earth's oceans.

surface is being altered by plastic production and highlights the fact that plastic does not biodegrade. The collections of plastic debris in the Great Pacific Garbage Patch and surrounding shorelines and the plastiglomerates found on beaches, such as those in Hawaii, can be fossilized into the future and can become part of Earth's strata. Another member of the study team, field archaeologist Dr. Matt Edgeworth, said, "It may seem odd to think of plastics as archaeological and geological materials because they are so new, but we increasingly find them as inclusions in recent strata. Plastics make excellent stratigraphic markers."[6]

No matter the name of the present geologic era, the impact of humans on Earth is undeniable. A study of Earth's gyres, conducted by scientists and researchers from around the world, revealed there is an estimated 300,000 short tons (270,000 metric tons) of debris in the oceans that comes from 5.25 trillion individual bits of debris.[7] There are also predictions that the Great Pacific Garbage Patch will double in size between 2012 and 2022. At the same time, by 2050, worldwide plastic production is predicted to quadruple to 2 trillion pounds (910 billion kg) per year.[8]

PLASTIC ENERGY

There are a few programs that turn plastic marine debris into energy, such as the Nets to Energy program in Hawaii dedicated to converting derelict fishing nets to energy. However, scientists have not yet figured out how to efficiently separate the different types of plastic in mainstream recycling programs, or how to separate plastic materials from nonplastic materials in order to convert the plastic into energy. But they are working on it. One study by the Earth Engineering Center of Columbia University in 2011 found that if the amount of energy inherent in discarded plastics could be recovered, it would be the equivalent of 139 million barrels of oil.[9] The study also looked at different ways the energy could be recovered, including converting plastics directly into liquid fuel, utilizing some plastics as fuel in certain types of power plants, and burning more garbage in waste-to-energy facilities.

Many people believe the best way to help the oceans is to prevent garbage from getting to them in the first place.

INTO THE FUTURE

Regardless of how the issue is framed, the Great Pacific Garbage Patch is an environmental problem of concern, and efforts that look at both cleanup and prevention may be the solution. Boyan Slat of the Ocean Cleanup said, "It is not a question of either cleanup or prevention. It's cleanup *and* prevention. If a cleanup started today, it would be a bit like mopping up the floor while the tap is still running. Prevention is absolutely essential. But until now, the mop hadn't been invented yet. The plastic trash that's out there won't go away by itself."[10] Prevention, according to Marcus Eriksen, captain of the JUNK sailboat, needs to focus on three areas. First, he says there needs to be increased education and awareness programs, as well as better litter laws. Next, Eriksen believes there needs to be improved waste management. Lastly, he would like to see greater responsibility placed on plastic producers.

GYRES MAY HAVE EXIT DOORS

The ocean's gyres, massive swirls of current, are thought to collect and concentrate debris in the vortex. A 2016 study by French oceanographers, however, revealed that while currents do concentrate the debris, they can eventually disperse it onto the shore through currents flowing away from the gyres. Computer models showed outward-bound currents flowing east toward North and South America. Some people saw this as good news for cleanup because organizers can optimize efforts based on this new knowledge. On the other hand, it created concern for marine life near the shore and coastal habitats, such as coral reefs and wetlands, because debris does more harm near the shore than it does in the open ocean.

One of the most prominent institutions focused on the Great Pacific Garbage Patch, the NOAA Marine Debris Program, has a bold strategic action plan in place to address and prevent marine debris. Its goals include coordinating marine debris efforts locally, nationally, and globally. NOAA helps prepare for and respond to emergency events, such as hurricanes and tsunamis, to lessen the impact of debris that ends up in the ocean. NOAA looks for ways to remove marine debris and works to educate people and change behaviors in order to prevent marine debris. NOAA also conducts continuing research and assessment of marine debris.

Of the marine debris in the Great Pacific Garbage Patch, most of it is plastic. It is designed to last forever, and many plastic products are made to be used only once, including bags and bottles. Marine debris education and awareness programs are working to create a cultural shift in how consumers use and dispose of plastic. Once demand for disposable plastics

Cleanup efforts to keep trash out of the oceans take place around the world.

decreases, the plastics industry will also need to make changes. Filmmaker Jo Ruxton, who produced the documentary *A Plastic Ocean* about the plastic debris in the world's gyres, believes public awareness can have an enormous impact. "If people realize how easy it is to make changes, and if they understand the consequences of not doing so, they want to change," Ruxton said.[11]

One way to reduce the number of plastic bags on Earth is to use reusable shopping bags instead.

There is optimism from many people that the Great Pacific Garbage Patch can be cleaned up or, at the very least, kept from growing so its harmful effects come under better control. This will require coordinated efforts between countries, groups, businesses, and individuals from around the world. "It's not a hopeless situation," said Dianna Parker of NOAA's Marine Debris Program. "Marine debris is absolutely a solvable problem because it comes from us humans and our everyday practices. We can take any number of steps to keep it from entering the ocean and that can happen at the highest level with governments and it can happen at the lowest level with individuals and everyday choices."[12]

"Plastic is in the air we breathe, it's become part of the soil and the animal kingdom. We're becoming plastic people."[13]
—*Captain Charles Moore, 2016*

CAUSE AND EFFECT

Increased plastic products

Nurdles

Improper waste disposal

Debris originates on land

Debris originates from ocean activities

Derelict fishing gear

Shipping losses

Gyre concentrates debris in Great Pacific Garbage Patch

Gyre deposits debris on shores

Degraded ocean habitats (oceans, coral reefs) → Fish and wildlife harmed → Ingestion / Entanglement

Degraded ocean habitats (oceans, coral reefs) → Loss of biodiversity

Fish and wildlife harmed → Loss of biodiversity

Degraded coastal habitats (beaches) → Degraded ocean habitats (oceans, coral reefs)

Degraded coastal habitats (beaches) → Loss of biodiversity

Degraded coastal habitats (beaches) → Birds and animals harmed

Degraded coastal habitats (beaches) → Humans impacted

Birds and animals harmed → Loss of biodiversity

Birds and animals harmed → Ingestion / Entanglement

Humans impacted → Recreation

Humans impacted → Health

Humans impacted → Safety

Humans impacted → Costs money

ESSENTIAL FACTS

WHAT IS HAPPENING

The Great Pacific Garbage Patch is not an island or a raft of trash; in fact, much of it can't be seen. Nonetheless, the North Pacific Gyre concentrates the marine debris in the Pacific Ocean in one area, which is growing in size. Part of the problem is the fact that the majority of the debris is plastic, which never biodegrades. Instead, it breaks down into smaller and smaller pieces. Fish, birds, turtles, dolphins, and all marine life are harmed by the debris, either by eating it or getting caught in it, and marine habitats are likewise damaged by the debris. Humans could also be at risk.

THE CAUSES

The Great Pacific Garbage Patch is the result of improper disposal of manufactured items that end up in the marine environment. They are concentrated in the swirling currents of the North Pacific Gyre. Eighty percent of all marine debris originates on land. The rest comes from activities at sea.

WHEN AND WHERE IT'S HAPPENING

The North Pacific Gyre concentrates the marine debris in the Pacific Ocean in one area. This is an ongoing problem with no end in sight. The concentration of debris stretches from the West Coast of North America all the way to Japan, and the problem is growing.

KEY PLAYERS

» Captain Charles Moore first encountered the Great Pacific Garbage Patch in 1997 and was appalled by what he saw. He is credited with bringing attention to the growing issue of marine debris and its effects on the oceans, marine life, and humans. Moore also founded Algalita, a nonprofit organization dedicated to mitigating the impacts of marine debris through research and education.

» The NOAA Marine Debris Program was created in 2006 through the Marine Debris Act. The mission of the program is to study and prevent the adverse effects of marine debris through action, education, debris removal, research, and the coordination of marine debris efforts locally, nationally, and globally.

» The plastics industry is one of the top industries in the United States. It produces billions of tons of plastic resin annually to manufacture plastic products that never fully biodegrade.

WHAT IT MEANS FOR THE FUTURE

At this point, scientists are not entirely sure about the long-term impacts of the Great Pacific Garbage Patch and others like it in the world's oceans. If the issue is not mitigated, it is clear marine habitats and wildlife will continue to suffer. The production of plastic has continued to grow, and the plastics industry is being called on to take responsibility for its products. This could include recovering plastics for recycling or energy production or producing plastics that are entirely biodegradable. As of 2017, there were cleanup efforts underway both on land and at sea. There were also massive public awareness campaigns urging people to change their habits and recycle plastic properly or use less of it. Until plastic entering the ocean can be stopped at the source, the Great Pacific Garbage Patch will continue to grow.

QUOTE

"It was and is a thin plastic soup, a soup lightly seasoned with plastic flakes, bulked out here and there with 'dumplings': buoys, net clumps, floats, crates, and other 'macro debris.'"

—*Captain Charles Moore*

GLOSSARY

anthropocene

Of or relating to the current geologic period, which focuses on the impact humans have on the environment.

biodiversity

The many different plants and animals in an ecosystem.

biomagnification

The process by which a compound, such as a pollutant or pesticide, increases its concentration in the tissues of organisms as it travels through the food web.

climate change

A process affecting the planet that is causing temperatures around the world to rise.

coalition

A collection of groups or people that have joined together for a common purpose.

derelict

Abandoned or discarded.

fossil fuel

A natural fuel, such as coal or gas, which contributes to global climate change.

hydrocarbon

A substance containing only hydrogen and carbon.

joint declaration

A formal announcement by two or more organizations.

municipal
Of or relating to cities.

phenomenon
An observed event, especially one with an unclear or unknown explanation.

plankton
Microscopic marine plant or animal life.

plastivore
A species that eats plastic.

sequester
To isolate from.

subtropical high
An area of semipermanent high pressure with warm, dry, calm weather.

synthetic
Made by humans.

zooplankton
Tiny floating animals that feed on phytoplankton.

ADDITIONAL RESOURCES

SELECTED BIBLIOGRAPHY

Algalita. Algalita Marine Research Foundation, n.d. Web. 21 Oct. 2016.

Moore, Captain Charles. *Plastic Ocean*. New York: Penguin, 2011. Print.

NOAA Marine Debris Program. US Department of Commerce, n.d. Web. 18 Oct. 2016.

Ocean Conservancy. Ocean Conservancy, n.d. Web. 31 Oct. 2016.

Plastic Paradise. Angela A. Sun, dir. Bullfrog Films, 2014. DVD.

FURTHER READINGS

Burns, Loree Griffin. *Tracking Trash: Flotsam, Jetsam, and the Science of Ocean Motion*. New York: Houghton, 2007. Print.

Decker, Julie. *Gyre: The Plastic Ocean*. London: Booth-Clibborn, 2014. Print.

Schier, Helga, and Lynn M. Zott, eds. *Endangered Oceans*. Farmington Hills, MI: Gale, 2014. Print.

WEBSITES

To learn more about Ecological Disasters, visit **abdobooklinks.com**. These links are routinely monitored and updated to provide the most current information available.

FOR MORE INFORMATION

For more information on this subject, contact or visit the following organizations:

Algalita

148 N. Marina Drive
Long Beach, CA 90803
562-598-4889
http://www.algalita.org/

Algalita is a nonprofit organization founded by Captain Charles Moore. It is made up of a small team of people who are dedicated to solving the marine debris problem through education and research.

Environmental Protection Agency's Trash-Free Waters Program

75 Hawthorne Street (SFD-9)
San Francisco, CA 94105
https://www.epa.gov/trash-free-waters

This program is working to reduce the amount of trash that enters all US waterways in an effort to lessen the impact on the environment, wildlife, and human health.

NOAA Marine Debris Program

marinedebris.web@noaa.gov
https://marinedebris.noaa.gov/

This program is run by the US government. It is the lead organization addressing the marine debris issue at a national and global level.

SOURCE NOTES

CHAPTER 1. THE GREAT PACIFIC GARBAGE PATCH

1. "Great Pacific Garbage Patch." *National Geographic*. National Geographic Society, n.d. Web. 18 Oct. 2016.

2. Captain Charles Moore. *Plastic Ocean*. New York: Penguin, 2011. Print. 48.

3. "Great Pacific Garbage Patch." *National Geographic*. National Geographic, n.d. Web. 18 Oct. 2016.

4. Troy Kitch. "The Great Pacific Garbage Patch." *Making Waves—NOAA Marine Debris Program*. US Department of Commerce, 26 June 2014. Web. 18 Oct. 2016.

5. Eric Hand. "Trillions of Plastic Pieces May Be Trapped in Arctic Ice." *Science*. American Association for the Advancement of Science, 22 May 2014. Web. 21 Oct. 2016.

6. Daniel Engber. "There Is No Island of Trash in the Pacific." *Slate*. Slate Group, 12 Sept. 2016. Web. Oct. 18 2016.

7. Captain Charles Moore. *Plastic Ocean*. New York: Penguin, 2011. Print. 2.

8. Laura Parker. "Plane Search Shows World's Oceans Are Full of Trash." *National Geographic*. National Geographic, 4 Apr. 2014. Web. 21 Oct. 2016.

9. Kurt Mann, prod. "Trash Talk: What Is the Great Pacific Garbage Patch?" *NOAA Marine Debris Program*. US Department of Commerce, n.d. Web. 18 Oct. 2016.

10. "Great Pacific Garbage Patch." *National Geographic*. National Geographic, n.d. Web. 18 Oct. 2016.

11. Richard A. Lovett. "Huge Garbage Patch Found in Atlantic Too." *National Geographic*. National Geographic, 2 Mar. 2010. Web. 21 Oct. 2016.

CHAPTER 2. A SHORT HISTORY OF TRASH

1. Sarah Bergen. "Green Film Exposes Society's Plastic Obsession." *Rider News*. Rider News, 16 Sept. 2014. Web. 28 Feb. 2017.

2. Marcia Anderson. "Confronting Plastic Pollution One Bag at a Time." *EPA Blog*. US Environmental Protection Agency, 1 Nov. 2016. Web. 3 Nov. 2016.

3. Ben Cosgrove. "'Throwaway Living': When Tossing Out Everything Was All the Rage." *Time*. Time, 15 May 2014. Web. 21 Oct. 2016.

4. Kieron Monks. "The Plastic Plague: Can Our Oceans Be Saved from Environmental Ruin?" *CNN World*. Cable News Network, 2 Sept. 2016. Web. 30 Oct. 2016.

5. "Seas of Plastic." *TED*. TED Conferences, Feb. 2009. Web. 3 Nov. 2016.

6. "Plastic Garbage Islands." *Visualeyed*. The Visual Agency, n.d. Web. 21 Oct. 2016.

7. Kurt Mann, prod. "Trash Talk: What Is the Great Pacific Garbage Patch?" *NOAA Marine Debris Program*. US Department of Commerce, n.d. Web. 18 Oct. 2016.

8. "Plastic Garbage Islands." *Visualeyed*. The Visual Agency, n.d. Web. 21 Oct. 2016.

9. "Great Pacific Garbage Patch." *National Geographic*. National Geographic, n.d. Web. 18 Oct. 2016.

10. Laura Parker. "Plane Search Shows World's Oceans Are Full of Trash." *National Geographic*. National Geographic, 4 Apr. 2014. Web. 21 Oct. 2016.

CHAPTER 3. IMPACT ON MARINE HABITATS

1. Mark McCormick. "How the Great Pacific Garbage Patch Is Destroying the Oceans and the Future for Marine Life." *One Green Planet*. One Green Planet, 4 Mar. 2015. Web. 21 Oct. 2016.

2. Captain Charles Moore. *Plastic Ocean*. New York: Penguin, 2011. Print. 109, 116.

3. Ibid.

4. Ibid. 118.

5. "How Does Marine Debris Impact Corals?" *NOAA Marine Debris Program*. US Department of Commerce, n.d. Web. 21 Oct. 2016.

6. "Take Action: Plastic Bottles." *More Ocean Less Plastic*. 5 Gyres Institute, n.d. Web. 21 Oct. 2016.

7. "Why Donate?" *Reef Check*. Reef Check Foundation, n.d. Web. 21 Oct. 2016.

8. Kenneth R. Weiss. "Altered Oceans Part Four: Plague of Plastic Chokes the Seas." *Los Angeles Times*. Los Angeles Times, 2 Aug. 2006. Web. 21 Oct. 2016.

9. Thomas M. Kostigen. *You Are Here*. New York: Harper, 2008. Print. 144.

CHAPTER 4. IMPACT ON FISH AND WILDLIFE

1. Captain Charles Moore. *Plastic Ocean*. New York: Penguin, 2011. Print. 121.

2. Mario Aguilera. "Scripps Study Finds Plastic in Nine Percent of 'Garbage Patch' Fishes." *Scripps Institution of Oceanography*. Scripps Institution of Oceanography, 30 June 2011. Web. 30 Oct. 2016.

3. Ibid.

4. 16X9 Global News. "Garbage Patch in the Middle of the Ocean." *YouTube*. YouTube, 9 Aug. 2012. Web. 18 Oct. 2016.

5. Sid Perkins. "Nearly Every Seabird May Be Eating Plastic by 2050." *Science*. American Association for the Advancement of Science, 31 Aug. 2015. Web. 25 Oct. 2016.

6. Laura Parker. "With Millions of Tons of Plastic in Oceans, More Scientists Studying Impact." *National Geographic*. National Geographic, 13 June 2014. Web. 30 Oct. 2016.

7. "Laysan Albatross." *Midway Atoll National Wildlife Refuge and Battle of Midway National Memorial*. US Fish and Wildlife Service, Web. 28 Feb. 2016.

8. "Plastic Garbage Islands." *Visualeyed*. The Visual Agency, n.d. Web. 21 Oct. 2016.

9. Sid Perkins. "Nearly Every Seabird May Be Eating Plastic by 2050." *Science*. American Association for the Advancement of Science, 31 Aug. 2015. Web. 25 Oct. 2016.

10. "The Marine Debris Act." *NOAA Marine Debris Program*. US Department of Commerce, n.d. Web. 30 Oct. 2016.

11. Joseph Stromberg. "How Plastic Pollution Can Carry Flame Retardants into Your Sushi." *Smithsonian*. Smithsonian, 21 Nov. 2013. Web. 8 Nov. 2016.

12. Kieron Monks. "The Plastic Plague: Can Our Oceans Be Saved from Environmental Ruin?" *CNN World*. Cable News Network, 2 Sept. 2016. Web. 30 Oct. 2016.

13. Sid Perkins. "Nearly Every Seabird May Be Eating Plastic by 2050." *Science*. American Association for the Advancement of Science, 31 Aug. 2015. Web. 25 Oct. 2016.

CHAPTER 5. IMPACT OF MARINE DEBRIS ON HUMANS

1. "Good Mate Green Boating." *Ocean Conservancy*. Ocean Conservancy, n.d. Web. 31 Oct. 2016.

2. "The Impacts of Mismanaged Trash." *EPA*. US Environmental Protection Agency, n.d. Web. 26 Oct. 2016.

3. Ibid.

4. "How Our Trash Affects the Whole Planet." *Green Living Ideas*. Sustainable Enterprises Media, n.d. Web. 26 Oct. 2016.

5. Ibid.

6. Nate Seltenrich. "New Link in the Food Chain? Marine Plastic Pollution and Seafood Safety." *Environmental Health Perspective* 123.2 (Feb. 2015). *National Institute of Environmental Health Sciences*. Web. 26 Oct. 2016.

7. Gaelle Gourmelon. "Global Plastic Production Rises, Recycling Lags." *Worldwatch Institute*. Worldwatch Institute, 28 Jan. 2015. Web. 25 Oct. 2016.

CHAPTER 6. MONITORING AND CLEANUP EFFORTS

1. TEDx Talks. "How the Oceans Can Clean Themselves: Boyan Slat." *YouTube*. YouTube, 24 Oct. 2012. Web. 27 Oct. 2016.

2. Ibid.

3. Ibid.

4. UPHIGH Productions. "Solar Powered 'Water Wheel' Behold The Future." *YouTube*. YouTube, 22 Jan. 2016. Web. 27 Oct. 2016.

5. "Learn the Facts." *Bag Monster*. Bag Monster, n.d. Web. 31 Oct. 2016.

6. "International Coastal Cleanup—2016 Report." *Ocean Conservancy*. Ocean Conservancy, n.d. Web. 31 Oct. 2016.

7. Ryan Tabata and Rhonda Suka. "Midway through Cleaning Up Midway Island." *Plastic Pollution Coalition*. PlasticPollutionCoalition. org. 18 May 2016. Web. 7 Nov. 2016.

8. "Videos: #6." *NOAA Marine Debris Program*. US Department of Commerce, 2016. Web. 31 Oct. 2016.

9. Kalyan Kumar. "The 'Great Pacific Garbage Patch' Is Bigger, Denser Than Earlier Thought." *Tech Times*. Tech Times, 7 Oct. 2016. Web. 27 Oct. 2016.

10. Mackenzie Anderson. "Great Things Come in Innovative Packaging: An Introduction to PlantBottle™ Packaging." *Coca Cola*. Coca Cola Company, 3 June 2015. Web. 27 Oct. 2016.

11. Recycling Today Staff. "ACC Announces Winners of Its 2015 Innovation in Plastics Recycling Awards." *Recycling Today*. GIE Media, 13 Nov. 2015. Web. 27 Oct. 2016.

12. Ibid.

13. Nathan Collins. "A Better Way to Clean Up Ocean-Polluting Plastics." *Pacific Standard*. Pacific Standard Magazine, 19 Jan. 2016. Web. 27 Oct. 2016.

CHAPTER 7. GARBAGE PATCH PREVENTION

1. *Plastic Paradise*. Angela A. Sun, dir. Bullfrog Films, 2014. DVD.

2. "Videos: #6." *NOAA Marine Debris Program*. US Department of Commerce, 2016. Web. 31 Oct. 2016.

3. Enjoli Francis. "California Strikes Down Proposal to Ban Plastic Bags." *ABC News*. ABC News, 1 Sept. 2010. Web. 31 Oct. 2016.

4. "2015 Report." *Ocean Conservancy*. Ocean Conservancy, n.d. Web. 31 Oct. 2016.

5. Steven Nelson. "Plastic Bag Lobby Intends to Blow Away California Ban." *US News and World Report*. US News and World Report, 2 Oct. 2014. Web. 3 Mar. 2017.

6. "Global Plastics Industry Activities to Prevent Marine Litter Grow to 260 Projects Worldwide." *Marine Litter Solutions*. Marine Litter Solutions, 20 May 2016. Web. 1 Nov. 2016.

7. Thomas M. Kostigen. *You Are Here*. New York: Harper, 2008. Print. 160.

8. Kieron Monks. "The Plastic Plague: Can Our Oceans Be Saved from Environmental Ruin?" *CNN World*. Cable News Network, 2 Sept. 2016. Web. 30 Oct. 2016.

9. "JUNK Raft-Old." *Marcus Eriksen*. Marcus Eriksen, n.d. Web. 10 Nov. 2016.

10. "America Recycles Day Report 2015." *America Recycles Day*. Keep America Beautiful, n.d. Web. 1 Nov. 2016.

11. Ibid.

12. "Plastic Garbage Islands." *Visualeyed*. The Visual Agency, n.d. Web. 21 Oct. 2016.

CHAPTER 8. THE OCEANS' FUTURE IN THE AGE OF PLASTIC

1. Angelicque E. White. "Research." *Interdisciplinary Oceanography*. Angelicque E. White, Web. 22 Feb. 2017.

2. Thomas M. Kostigen. *You Are Here*. New York: Harper, 2008. Print. 144.

3. "Great Pacific Garbage Patch." *National Geographic*. National Geographic, n.d. Web. 18 Oct. 2016.

4. Kathryn Potraz. "Plastic Permanence: Our Litter Is Now Part of the Geologic Record." *Sierra*. Sierra Club, 22 July 2014. Web. 3 Nov. 2016.

5. Sarah Knapton and Jonathan Pearlman. "'Great Pacific Garbage Patch' Is a Myth, Warn Experts, as Survey Shows There Is No 'Rubbish Island.'" *Telegraph*. Telegraph Media Group, 5 Oct. 2016. Web. 3 Nov. 2016.

6. "Human Impact Has Created a 'Plastic Planet'—Anthropocene Study into Lasting Effects of Plastic on Land and Oceans." *Science Daily*. Science Daily, 27 Jan. 2016. Web. 3 Nov. 2016.

7. The 5 Gyres Institute. "First Global Estimate of Plastic Pollution in Our Oceans." *YouTube*. YouTube, 24 Mar. 2016. Web. 3 Nov. 2016.

8. *Plastic Paradise*. Angela A. Sun, dir. Bullfrog Films, 2014. DVD.

9. Renee Cho. "What Happens to All That Plastic?" *State of the Planet*. Earth Institute—Columbia University, 31 Jan. 2012. Web. 3 Nov. 2016.

10. Julie Dugdale. "The Ocean Cleanup Plan So Crazy It Just Might Work." *Outside*. outsideonline.com, 21 July 2015. Web. 22 Feb. 2017.

11. Kieron Monks. "The Plastic Plague: Can Our Oceans Be Saved from Environmental Ruin?" *CNN World*. Cable News Network, 2 Sept. 2016. Web. 30 Oct. 2016.

12. Troy Kitch. "The Great Pacific Garbage Patch." *Making Waves—NOAA Marine Debris Program*. US Department of Commerce. 26 June 2014. Web. 18 Oct. 2016.

13. Kieron Monks. "The Plastic Plague: Can Our Oceans Be Saved from Environmental Ruin?" *CNN World*. Cable News Network, 2 Sept. 2016. Web. 30 Oct. 2016.

INDEX

ABOUT THE AUTHOR

Laura Perdew is an author, writing consultant, former middle school teacher, self-admitted tree hugger, and lifelong supporter of the reduce, reuse, recycle philosophy. She writes fiction and nonfiction for children, including many titles for the education market. Perdew lives and plays in Boulder, Colorado. She is the author of *Kids on the Move! Colorado*, a guide to traveling through Colorado with children.